Words My Father Gave Me

Mahogany Jones

BookLeaf Publishing

India | USA | UK

Presentation by *BookLeaf Publishing*

Web: www.bookleafpub.com

E-mail: info@bookleafpub.com

ISBN: 9789360946548

First edition 2024

In Dedication to Joan, Roy, and Nanette.

You are missed and still felt.

ACKNOWLEDGEMENT

I am deeply grateful to all those who have supported and inspired me throughout the creation of this collection of poems.

Thank you, God, for being the illest poet to ever compose. Thank you for your friendship and guidance through the years, thank you for your love, grace, and brilliance.

Thank you to my Husband, Dre, for his unwavering love and encouragement. Your presence in my life has been a source of strength and inspiration. You have managed to hold me down and keep me lifted in the most remarkable of ways, I love you, babe. To my babies, Ellie, Jaz, AJ and ViVi, thank you—I love you more than you know. You are constantly teaching me, and you each have blessed me beyond measure. My Mom, my Uncle and Cousins—love you guys!

To my friends, know that I deeply appreciate you. Your companionship has been a constant source of joy and comfort and I'm blessed to have you. You have been my chosen family.

Your love has given me the freedom I needed to lean into being my best self.

To my mentors and teachers. Your wisdom and guidance has not only shaped my journey as a poet, but an educator, and human. Thank you for fueling my passion for writing and for living.

To my readers and listeners, I want to extend my sincerest gratitude for engaging in my work, offering feedback, encouragement, and lending me your hearts along the way. Your presence and enthusiasm have fueled my creativity along the way. You are appreciated.

PREFACE

Growing up, I didn't have the privilege to create a real relationship with my Father. The last time I saw him face to face, I was six. The last time we spoke I was nine.

However, for the short period of time with him in my life, he would tell me the coolest riddles, and recite some of the best poetry.

Those who knew my Father would tell me I looked just like him. However, what I am most grateful for inheriting from his bloodline has to be my relationship with words.

I am truly in love with words, stories, and the space the page has so generously provided me down through the years to be myself. Poetry has not only been about the art form, but poetry has been both a friend and healer.

With 'Words My Father Gave Me,' I am inviting you to navigate an intricate maze of love and loss, hope and despair.

As you delve into these "verses," I hope you find solace in the echoes of your own journey. I hope you discover resonance in your own story.

These poems are part commemoration and celebration of a life well-lived, one that I am grateful to still be alive to figure out.

Thank you for joining me for the ride.

For Joan, Nanette, and Roy

The women in my family
are
Big Body
Whip pushers
We are pistol-totin'
Women
Women who shoot at cheatin' first husbands
but take fist to mouth
from second ones

The women in my family
are
Cymbal crashing
Brash
Women
Our saunters full of sashay Old Bay and juju
Our laughter full of
"Nigga please"
and
"I wish you would"

We are Bermuda Triangular
Women
The kind you get lost inside of
The kind who will sadly lose themselves

Forget they are
Airbender
and
Firestarter

We are women who spent lifetimes behind
Park Ave penthouse bolts
and
penitentiary bars
All to keep the world shut out
Keep ourselves shut in.

Choosing to die alone and that being just fine.

We are women who say the right thing
At the right time.

Women who make rice pudding from scratch
Fill up apartments with cardamom and safety.

We are women whose arms you come home to.

We are cashmere trench coat-drenched
Cartier wrist-watched
Caramel-colored Italian leather tote bagged

Women with class

Praying women
Who have been preyed upon by pimps and
pastors and pastors who were pimps

Women

Women
Who afterlife consumed them
Managed to claw their way up out of life's
esophagus.
We are gouged-out-eyed Samsons
Shorn locked with one good fight left in them
Women

Women
Full of wonder and beauty.

Elle

My heart is 37 inches tall,
wildly wanders into every room I happen to be
in, and giggles at random.
She is a warrior's song full of vibrant and perfect
syncopation.
She is 1,046 days old and at random she will
rattle off a list of the planets
Almost always placing her name immediately
after Neptune—she knows.
I take more pictures of her than I'm sure I
should—
6,542, according to i-cloud—I know
I take the chaos of her wonder for granted.
I try to form my palms into the shape of bowls
attempting to hold enough rain to taste.
Time falls heavy and steady—
I barely manage to hold her hand—let alone our
moments.
The doctors tell me she is in the 93rd percentile
of children her age for her height,
I can't wait to loiter in the shadow of all she
becomes.

Response to Brittnay Rogers
... "I imagine giving birth is a rebellion"

My amniotic sac and pelvic floor
Atlantic
ancestral collective resistance
rallying the troops
my ovaries assembling
my body, army of one
my swollen abdomen
Trojan
horse
for months you are
part secret, part weapon,
IUD,
welcomed invasion
landmine
obliterating
all I once knew
myself
to be
revolutionizing all
of who I will
become.

Let Me Be

Let me be to language
What fire and straightening
comb be to nape of neck
bedazzled by naps

Let me be
Lay it down

These words in my mouth be scratch
to the itch of your dandruff scalp
These words rat tail comb
Divide and conquering

One part at a time
Index fingertip blue

Magic
Drip
Slather
Soothe

You sit with your eyes closed
Loose necked

Relaxed, bottom propped up on stacked floor
pillows
Your winged elbow propped up and positioned
just so
Nestled in my thigh meat with your frame
In between my legs

Use these words
like that comb to reach your in-betweens

Where you first misplaced yourself
In between the cracks

The words
small enough
to get to where it's been
too hard to reach

These words spacious
and cushioned
just enough
for the burden lay

These words
just enough
sprawl to be
rest for your weary

For Keeps

winding clocks
my hips tick and keep time
keep rhythm
keep nations
keep
i train them to let go
and
keep on
and
they do
it's in the letting go i learned love
thought i had to hold on
to him who wouldn't hold back
always held back
my back
press and comb
bone straight
i step into red patent leather pumps the same
way i climb into my sexy
and
conquer the night
color my skin constellations
look into my eyes and predict the future
i plant beds of lavender and gardenia in the good
soil of my crazy

and sane
give myself permission to not have to be
explained
or solved.
unresolved
untamed
won't ever let your storm dissolve my sugar
sweet.
i savor my taste
the way my shadow lingers
its resolve to remain unmoved
i used to collect eyes
used them to see out of, as if my vision needed
correction
i have given them back
slow explosion
fast collision
let me slide into this space that's here for me.
i'm here for me.
i'm here
i hear

listen.

Ode to Detroit

Buried alive by blight and bankruptcy.
It wasn't long ago we were all coated in the
ashen rubble of economic collapse.
Dazed and bewildered—
because
when skyscrapers of borrowed "not enoughs"
fall on you,
you're not expected to survive.
How did we survive?
Like we always have—
Together.
MawMaw's and PawPaw's
Abuela's and Abueltos,
Baba's and Umi's,
would have hot meals ready
and a little extra to hold you over
until payday—
(Even though you both knew it would be a long
time until that day came)
Uber before there was Uber
Do hair
Clean homes
Make dinners
until we could
"make due"

Because this is
what we do
Start-up businesses
When the world tries to
shut us out
shut us down
shut us up
until we quietly
"Move to where there's work."
But we make it work,
Like we always have,
Together.
I walk through Dequindre Cut,
along the Riverwalk,
ride the QLine,
take strolls downtown on Woodward
walk past
Detroit is the New Black
Think of how we were so
black
sheep
Now we're
so sheik
So
"Noir"
So right now
Revitalization never comes
assembled or "put together" ready
It doesn't even come with all the parts

or a package of government bail-out
Our economic renewal came with
bootstraps
us coming
Together
To engineer
our
come up
our
rise up
our
push through
we know what it's like to
push through
and pass
darkness
don't call it a
'Comeback'
We have been here
Learning how to stand after
losing a few limbs
and we are stabilizing
slowly getting our stride back
our bones ache with
it
we can see the fist-sized cloud
and smell the scent
new day and change
that's about to downpour.

Can't you feel it?
Together
working on our financial wellness nursing
ourselves back to the land of milk and honey
Overflow
Cheeks rosy with prosperity.
It's true
we ran out of money
But
We
didn't run out
We
stayed
mastered how to ration
a lifetime supply
of ingenuity
imagination
and
innovation.
The moon must hang low over you
Detroit
Your tide is rising
You are swelling
with new wave
of creatives, co-work spaces,
eateries, community gardens,
and solution.
An answer to the enigma of you.
Like Frida

taking the fractured cast of your broken and shed
body
And making it canvas
Making it art.
Detroit
We are stone mountain of
insurmountable
we are chiseling ourselves into a monument of
indomitable.

For The Birds

I sat and slowly lifted pad Thai to my mouth,
Chewed on what happened
in an attempt to masticate her nerve
and swallow my shame.
I chewed long enough to make all the ways I felt
displaced go down easier.
Her (with an angry stance and stank tone):
"Can I ask you a question—"
Me: (shocked) *silence*
Her: "Is there any reason why you keep looking
at my car?"
I never gave her permission to ask me a
question.
It was as if I now needed permission to have
my eyes
my body
on the same street
as
her car
her—
Thought to myself
(Without permission)
If you're so worried about your car
on this street
in this city

Maybe your car shouldn't be
on this street
in this city
If you don't think it's safe
here
Don't think
I'm safe
Me and my looks
have the right to
gaze and take in
You
Your car
Sun, moon, stars, and all of this green earth
Me and my look see all through you
and your misplaced attitudinal wanna be
bravado.
Me and my look locate every story you ever
heard about DETROIT,
About Black
About theft
About strong Black woman
"Sy Thai... I'm looking for Sy Thai"
I chewed and swallowed
"Love is patient. Love is kind...It is not rude... It
is not easily angered (this anger didn't come with
ease God)
It keeps no record of wrong. (God I keep trying
to get rid of these tired ol' songs in my head)."

When quietly the melody of tweets filled my
hearing.
The sweetness of a little bird helped themselves
to the seat opposite of me,
As if to remind me she wasn't afraid to share
space with me.
Soon I had a flock of tiny dinner guests.
We broke bread together as I shared my noodles
and eggs and peas and peace with them.
They accepted.
They knew I belonged there
In the heart of our city

They never once asked me
about their cars.

I've been feeling hot and angry, where do I put my gorgeous tender?

I will lie my gorgeous tender down in the river
pray for the Egyptian daughter to find it
and place it in palace
where it belongs
protected from a Pharaoh
who will want to slaughter
it
because it
is
first born
deliverer
"Let my people go…"

Salvation

I tuck my gorgeous tender in the crevices of my
smile
plaster it to seal the cracks of my lips that are
covered by my mask where it is
safe and unseen
hidden and protected
unlike me—

"Essential Worker"
over exposed and exploited
necessary and needed
until

not

knots—my gorgeous tender remembers
the 'forget me not's' of nooses
knows the disdain the world feels for the
magnificence of her beauty
it
will always be its desired bounty.
My gorgeous tender knows she is endangered.

but I don't want to put her away anymore
I refuse to ride in it
'gentle and unassuming.'

I want to put my gorgeous tender in thunder and
crack hemisphere

I want my to make my gorgeous tender deluge
and drown
and divide the continents again.
I want to put it in the air and infect
bloodstreams.

We are tired

and this is
ENOUGH.

Black is like...

Black pride smells
like red clay Mississippi baked in summertime
and blues
smells like
peach cobbler with thick thick crust and protest
My Home
taste of "Water to Win" and "Make it do it what
do" gourmet.

I become art
and
look like pyramid
look like innovation
look like
what's next
and
what's right
Now.

Racism feels like
not having a seat at the table you built

To own something sounds like how freedom
tastes—fresh

We know Jesus by His first name—
We understand suffering all too well—
We are very familiar with the miracle of making
due
We know holy
We Mary Magdalene
experts in
cleaning what treads over us with surrender
tender and tears

We study providing sight
The whole world blind to our plight—
Finally starting to see
We are ashes to ashes
Dust to dust
Red earthen vessels
Molded by God's hand
Shaped in His image for sure
We too are invisible but mighty

Try us and find out.

The Life of a Dream

If you want to understand
the life of a dream
Go to the water
Stand at the vastness of ocean
Your small frame wedged in between earth and
sky
And look at how each molecule
Assembled together
to become a body to live inside.
Make your dream something to live inside
Real dreams don't die
Dreams just are—
Origins rooted only in being and becoming
Dreams only exist in what always was, the right
now and what's next
You are what has always been
What is right now
And what's to come.
If a dream does die—
It doesn't rot like decomposing flesh
Doesn't have the ceremonial of whirling ravens
or flies ready to feast on its carcass
No
Dying dreams are more like dirty baseboards,
graying walls that once were gleaming white,

dying dreams are the dullness of withering
neglect
Dying dreams are destinies denied
Hopes deferred
When you dream a dream
Wake up
Write it down
Call your grandma
Make sense of it
But whatever you do—
Don't forget
The living of a dream is in the remembering
We can't afford to forget
Live like the forgotten
Careless
With no ambition
We are what dreams are made of
Darkness and magic
Marker
God's sentence etch sketched possibilities of
what can come true
What is a dream if not the ancestral linger
Of Holy Ghost
We an army of valley of resurrected dry bones
A battalion of light
Our great great great grandfather's clap back
You thought water hoses, batons, nooses,
Rabid dogs tearing at our flesh like children's
hands do when shredding construction paper

could keep our arms from extending and
handing bending to grip what's divinely ours?
We know all about doing this for hours
Hours that extended to
382 days of boycotting buses we weren't
allowed to sit in the front of—
We'd rather walk anyway
Rather stand anyway
Who has time to sit down
When your very legacy is being stomped out?
See dreams need the rhythm of our in and out
Life spans beyond bullet
and the great beyond
Dreams that make homes in the mind's eye of
our children's children.
What kills a dream is the letting go
Get your dream and hold on so tight that the
flesh of it lives under your fingernails
Clench down so tough that the remnants are
stuck in your teeth
The drippings of it on the corners of your mouth
Jaw locked tighter than your fist full of refusal to
let go.
Don't let go
You are the telling on the mountain
You are the wading and water and proof that we
got over
You are good news
Walking monument

Make sure you are the dream
Alive
Keep living
Alive
Dream.

And... I Still Do

You
are my love letter
and
I am yours.

Kiss me
on top

on top
of
ferris wheels
merry go rounds
counters
roofs
mounds of bills
mundane Monday's
moods and mishaps
the unsurmountable
and
every unmet expectation

we kiss
and
become
our desire

fulfilled

I invite you to
fill me
you
fill in my blanks
with the right answer
every time
even
when we are wrong
we
trace
erase
re-create
start over
loving one another in pencil

practicing the right ways to permeate
pleasure
persistence
going the distance lives in the consistent
we are learning the mastery
of practice making perfect
with every stroke
we are lifetime
extraordinary

permanent

Let's play 20 questions
for the next 20 years
knowing that we are
one another's answer
for each 20 questions
for 20 lifetimes

"we will figure it out"
is our love language
we are simple
and
complicated
but it's simple
I did
You did
so we
do
and
always will

I do
a way of being
a state
of mind
you are my homeland
and I am becoming familiar with our windings
and your back roads
I am proud to have you stake your
flag in me

even prouder to pledge
allegiance to our united.

circa 1995- For My Day Ones and the One Who Always Knew

We were
"Road Furniture"
posted up every weekend
along
125th St
West 4th
Al B Square Mall.
We were
15
16
17
We were
TOOOOOOO cute
underaged
and
overdressed
and
poorly supervised.
We were
"Hey Chocolate"
"Hey LightSkinned"

(for sure more "Hey Lightskinned"s, cause it
was the 90's and well we weren't as evolved and
self-loving as we are now)
and most importantly
We were
determined.
Determined to fill our
pockets
phone books
and
egos
with options.
I was 16 and finally allowed to see streetlights
pressed against the canvas of a blue-black sky
and a Moonlit Harlem—
so it was
"on and poppin"

It was Spring Break
with a Spring that hadn't quite sprung
so that night we all rocked our
"Triple Fat Gooses"
"Skullies"
"Wheat Timbos"
We decided
to find the
cheapest
darkest
brown liquor we could afford

from a bodega that would overlook my baby
face in exchange for my woman-like stature.
E&J it was
and we
poured some out
for the dead homies we didn't have
cause
we were
too young
too Middle Classed
too two parented homed
too Westchester
too Brooklyn Brownstone
too World Trade
to have
"dead homies"
But we'd pour some out anyway...
but
not too much
cause we needed to get...
wasted
drunk DRUNK
buttttttt
not so drunk that my Grandma could tell.
But
she could tell—
after cheek hugging cold concrete
while singing TLC's
"What about yooooooooo friendsssss'

I picked myself up
staggered into the lobby
attempted to avert the stares of the bellmen
made it to the elevator
and
coached myself:
"Self-walk straight—we straight."

"Hi Grandma"
"Hi Ressie"
"Ressie, hang up your coat."
The request made in the most suspicious of
tones
"Ressie—"
"Yeah Grandma?"
"Are you DRUNK?!?"
"What Grandma? Meeeee? Of course NOT!
Thought to myself—she knows—how does she
know?
"Grandma, I'm just tired. I'm gonna take a bath."
Soaking in guilt and adventure.
The soles of my feet and fingertips wrinkled in
intoxication.
One hour later, I yell from the bathtub
"Grandma, I'm drunk"
She laughed
but never told my Mother.

Man, I miss her.

She died two days after that
and I truly miss her
"knowing."

She always knew...

The Ancestry of Normal

How did we lose
Normal?
Moving in crowded spaces
Moving too fast
We stopped holding hands
and we haven't been the same since.
It's not like we were ever
American pie
but
we were warm
and
down home
in our way.
We had our own
way.
Somewhere along it
we
got lost
in exchange for normal
and I've been sad ever since.
I've never stopped
ever since.
I've never been
still enough
long enough

to feel the wet of tears on my cheeks
ever since
you
died—
I've lost
"just drop in's"
and
train rides home.

I wish I could give back some of these
"I remembers"
I have way too many
Always popping up reminding me all, all that I
don't have
especially you.
No
Grandma's hands
Grandma's face
Grandma's laugh
Grandma's Doublemint and Chanel
Grandma's "It's Ok"

Grandma
It's ok
I don't understand
I don't like it
But I understand
You were tired
We know

you tried.
Mommy misses you most
She is a ghost
a fraction
of who she used to be
a shell...
I try to get close
to see if I can hear the ocean
she is an echo.

We lost normal
the moment we lost
you.

Long Distance

Bad directions
It's always been difficult to pinpoint you
It's hard to find you
and I guess I never have had a good sense of
direction to begin with.
Sometimes I wonder if it's me—
Maybe I initially came with a set of instructions
that neither of us bothered to read.
I think
how many times we have assembled and
deconstructed one another's parts—
apart
Even when we are in the same room
Even when we had to sleep in the same room
and share the same bed
you managed to be
far-away
Not the kind of far-away
"like where's the remote"
out of reach kinda far
but
the kind where I have to wonder if I have
enough
for the flight
the kind of far away

that one has to learn a few phrases to manage.
You are a language
one I am not familiar with
Grandma always felt more
Mother tongue to me
You hardly ever spoke.
Numb
You
disconnected.
Your phone has been off and it's been 4 years to
date.
I'm not sure if I hate that we don't keep in touch
or
that you are just so out of it.

A Palm's Sunday

I have used my hands to...

hold my peace
disturb it
hold on to my last nerve
feed giraffes
hold my mother's hand when her mother, my
grandmother, died
let go of those who didn't deserve to have their
palms in mine
wash feet
jerk off teenage boys who I felt guilty for giving
them "blue balls" because I wouldn't give all the
way in
wipe away hot tears and sadness and rage when I
did
give in
all the way

I have used my hands to...
pray
pry open untruths in efforts to pen my own paths
to freedom
clean, season, flour, and fry chicken—good and
hard

touch stoves I knew were too hot because it just
might have been worth it
(rarely has it ever been)
rub salve on open wounds hoping to heal others
when I needed healing most
grip and Black girl stitch hair to scalp
hold myself together

I pray my palms memorize
the small of my lover's back
the prayers I have prayed for him while folding
his underwear
the imprint of my children's palms
and the prayer I have prayed for them while
making their beds
my destiny
and all the prayers I have prayed for myself

I wash my hands in hopes my palms will
forget
the weight of carrying the burdens of others for
too long
forget
the wait of waiting for someone, or any one to
see it was all
too much
like carrying
too many
grocery bags at once

we are never meant to attempt to carry
too much

I am still washing my hands in hopes my palms
forget
those who let my hand go when I needed them
the most
those who relinquished me
when I needed to be claimed
the most
those who let my hand go
left me to drown
when I needed
saving

I am teaching my wrist
to shift
to turn
to position
not just my palms
but my heart
upright
to not only pray
but to surrender
ask for assistance

I am teaching my heart to mindful
to know

it
and
we
are worth saving.

"I Sing The Body Electric"

my body has been
part truck, part spaceship
part fighter jet, part cathedral,
part
burial ground—
transporting the exotic
practicing the sacred
rituals of excavating exhumed
remains of a promise

my body
is a promise
that God gave my mother
without
giving her to me.

A Postpartum Covid

i
Haymakers of my now elongated breast
are being whipped out
to save the day
and my students' eardrums
from shrieks of my insatiable
1 year old.
We are virtual now
everything is
work
school
church
parties
our realities
relegated to bandwidth and frequencies
we all are
screen protectors
overexposed
we all wear
the mask
but there are still
some things you can't hide behind
I have decided
I am done with hiding
over feeling trapped

I have made plans
that one day
while at mall
or
Walmart
before the world opens back up
that I'm going to strip
take it all off
one day while I'm in the frozen food section
meal prepping in my head
that I'm going to bare it all
it's all been too much

ii
and though it's way quieter than
it's ever been
I miss silence
it was
hymnal
and
a bowed posture
it was
my journal
and a pen that skated figure 8's across pages
I miss the silence
I could fill it with everything that I didn't have
room for
now—
cries

and
dirty diapers
and all that's happening outside of me that's out
of my control

iii
I just want to be loved
one foot in front of the other
my body
a small factory
manufacturing
forward motion
and
muscle memory
my daughter
strapped to my chest
we are
in sync
there is a soft rhythm that happens in the pocket
of our bounce
it's beautiful
outside
and that reminds me
I'm beautiful
and it's one of the most pleasant things I've felt
on the inside
for a while
after a month of Sundays
of not feeling

beautiful.
I can't see the cardinals
but I feel them
God
scoops extra sun
and sprinkles stratus clouds
across the morning
the sweetness of this
marshmallow over my mundane is everything
and I am grateful.

Waning

See
the Moon
brimming over,
dripping with resolve
Unphased
and
waning crescent
refusing to give so much of herself
she has learned not to come to the table
too full
she has learned
her turns pull the tides of
seas worldwide
so she isn't phased when
a mere mortal turns his neck in her direction
attempting to drown their egos in her glow.

See
the Boy
his britches
2 sizes smaller
than his capacity
to maintain
a relationship that will last
longer than his wanderlust.

The Moon
anticipating
to be found
and
the boy
with his desire
to be
the first
to glide across.

See
the Table
set for two.
Both
the Moon
and
it
decorated perfectly
in white and waiting

both
the Table
the Moon
have witnessed
lovers
who
lose

Both
the Boy
and
the Moon
know
the end of this tale
before it's even
begun.

"Check Please."

Decluttering

Old mail
Any items acquired in Nepal
If it doesn't bring joy
If you haven't used it in a year
If you settle/tolerate it
If it makes you feel lack
If it's served it's time
If you aren't going to read it
If it's a mess
This mandate is applicable to the list mentioned
above
and
to all of the nouns that attach themselves to
being alive
any noun leaving you dead
on the inside
every single
person
place
and object
and especially the abstract ones
when love decides to show up in your
conversation as a noun
when love is no longer the vibrant verb of eyes
that sparkle when they land on you

toss it
throw it away
when it is now just the pretty box
big and bulky
dismantle it
tear down and deconstruct every abstract noun
that no longer serves
hate
unforgiveness
throw away all the pictures
if the way you are framed in them is anything
less than perfect
if it's too tight
if you've been waiting too long
if they have been on your phone for over 10
years and you met and spoke once
it was just a moment
you have what you needed
what's the residue
why the need for such objects
discard
make space
for
joy
for
new
for
more
more

more

more

more

more

more

The Becoming

When the sky is full of moon,
and you have made up your mind to carve your
initials into her thigh
this is when you hunt.
Search
your pockets
your cupholders
your jars
and you gather
every penny.

Then
search
all the wishing wells and fountains
within a 20-mile radius.

Consider
which penny belongs to
which well
which fountain.

Consider
which penny is
responsible
responsible

enough to carry
the burdens of each unreasonable and insatiable
desire.

Turn
your palms
face up

massage
the tips of your fingers.

Prepare
them for the scared

Make sure
your fingertips
know
know how to carry dreams.

Make sure
your fingertips are familiar
familiar with lightwork.

Make sure
your fingertips
know
know how to pray
and
get a prayer through

Make sure
your fingertips
UNDERSTAND.

Understand
that you being
80% water

are the wishing
and the well.

Use
fingertips to stir
stir the brew of your being.

Pour
out your
pennies
and
wishes
and
dreams
and
burdens
around you.

Sit
in your center

until you gurgle and swell
baptism
and
resurrection

Sit
until you
become
both
amen
and
so be it.

www.ingramcontent.com/pod-product-compliance
Lightning Source LLC
LaVergne TN
LVHW021237200726
843509LV00012B/1507